2017 GREATEST POP & MOVIE HITS

ARRANGED BY
DAN COATES

CONTENTS

Produced by
Alfred Music
P.O. Box 10003
Van Nuys, CA 91410-0003
alfred.com

Printed in USA.

ISBN-10: 1-4706-3878-9
ISBN-13: 978-1-4706-3878-8

Cover Image:
Red star: © iStock.com / dianaarturovna

7 YEARS

Words and Music by Lukas Forchhammer,
Morten Ristorp Jensen, Stefan Forrest, David Labrel,
Morten Pilegaard and Christopher Brown
Arr. Dan Coates

5

7

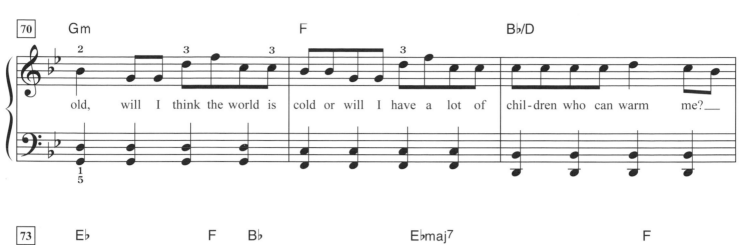

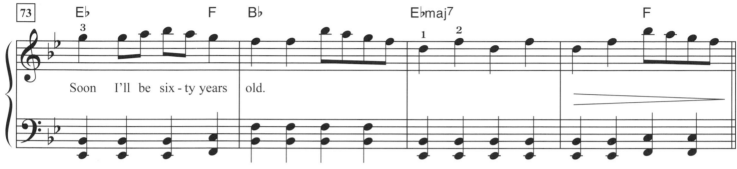

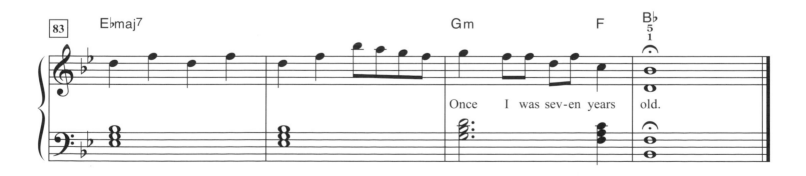

BLIND PIG

(from *Fantastic Beasts and Where to Find Them*)

Written by J.K. Rowling and Mario Grigorov
Arr. Dan Coates

9

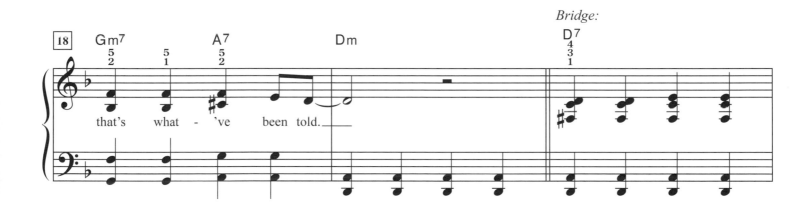

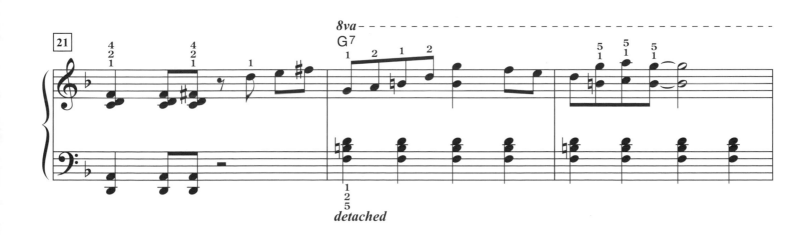

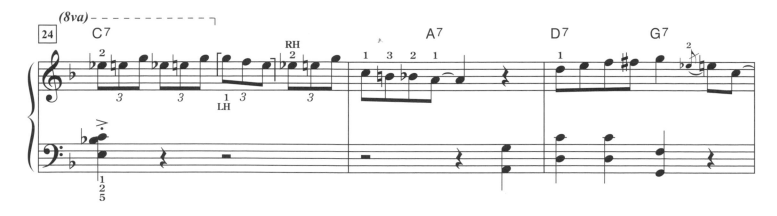

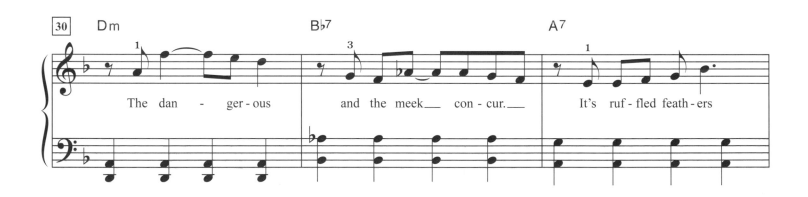

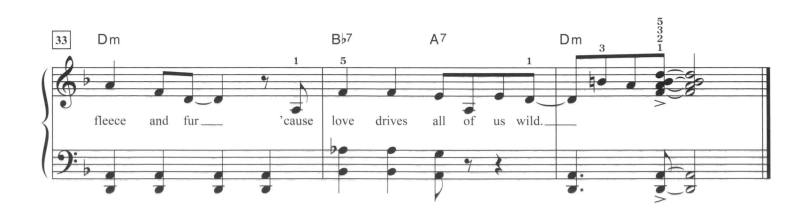

BLUE AIN'T YOUR COLOR

Words and Music by Steven Lee Olsen,
Clint Lagerberg and Hillary Lindsey
Arr. Dan Coates

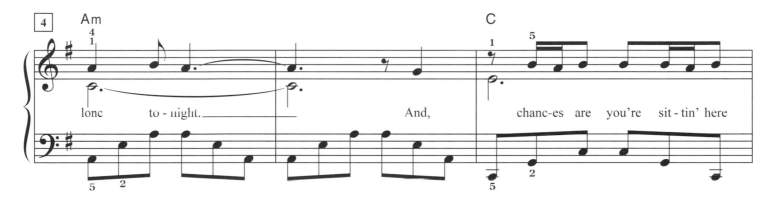

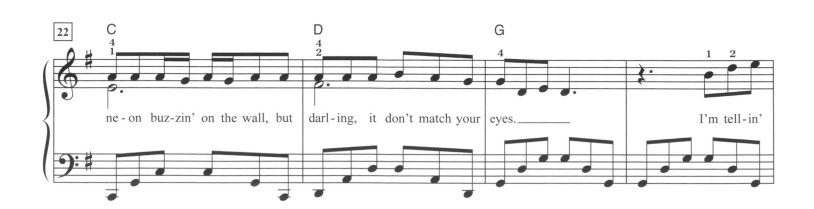

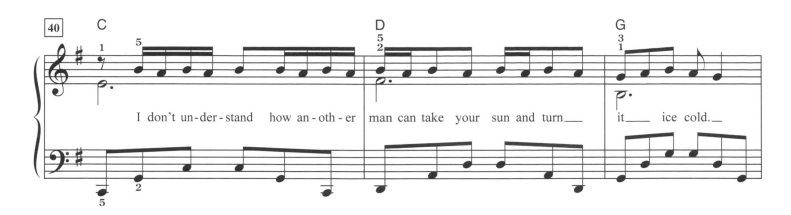

I don't un-der-stand how an-oth-er man can take your sun and turn___ it___ ice cold. __

Well, I've___ had e-nough to drink, and it's mak-in' me think that I

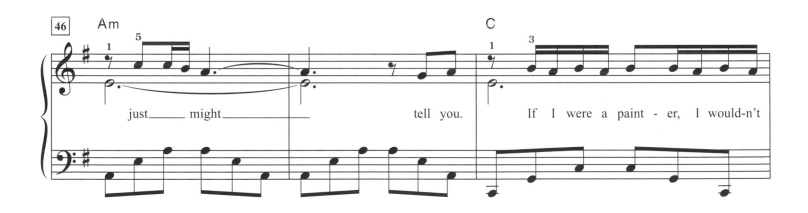

just___ might___ tell you. If I were a paint - er, I would-n't

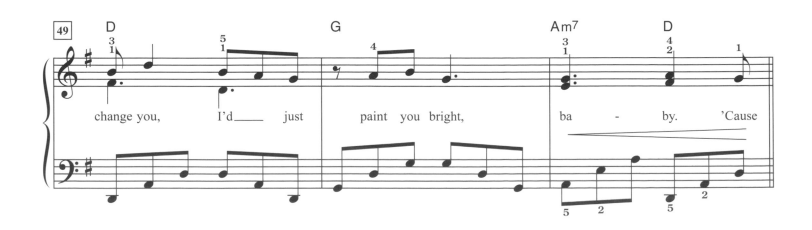

change you, I'd___ just paint you bright, ba - by. 'Cause

Chorus:

blue_____ looks good on the sky, looks good on that

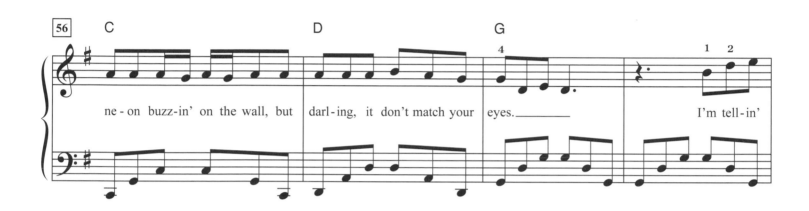

ne-on buzz-in' on the wall, but darl-ing, it don't match your eyes._____ I'm tell-in'

you,_____ you don't need that guy._____ It's so black and

white,___ he's steal-in' your thun-der,___ ba-by, blue ain't your col-or.

CHAINED TO THE RHYTHM

Words and Music by Katy Perry, Max Martin,
Sia Furler, Ali Payami and Skip Marley
Arr. Dan Coates

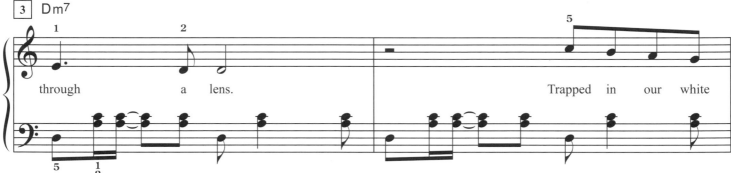

18

CLOSER

Words and Music by Shaun Frank, Andrew Taggart,
Isaac Slade, Ashley Frangipane and Frederic Kennett
Arr. Dan Coates

CITY OF STARS

(from *La La Land*)

Music by Justin Hurwitz
Lyrics by Benj Pasek & Justin Paul
Arr. Dan Coates

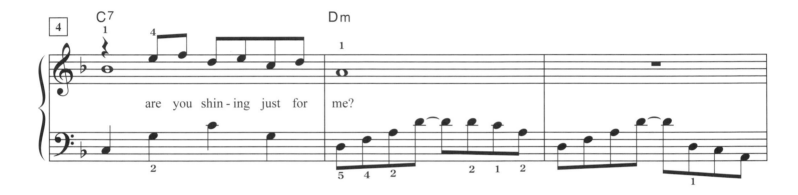

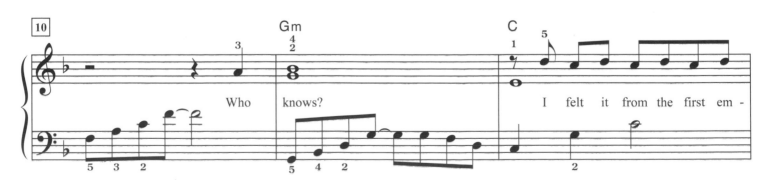

DON'T WANNA KNOW

Words and Music by Kendrick Lamar, Adam Levine,
Ammar Malik, John Ryan, Jacob Kasher Hindlin,
Alex Ben-Abdallah, Kurtis McKenzie and Jon Mills
Arr. Dan Coates

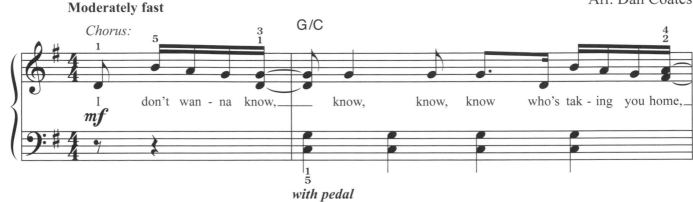

33

THE GREATEST

Words and Music by Kendrick Lamar,
Sia Furler and Greg Kurstin
Arr. Dan Coates

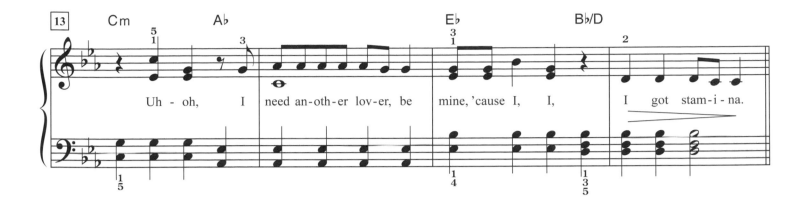

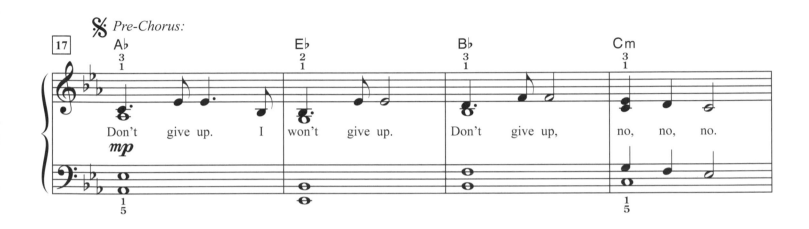

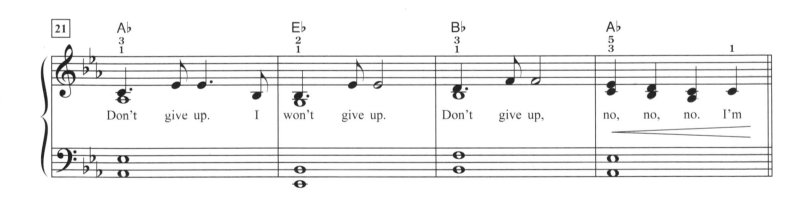

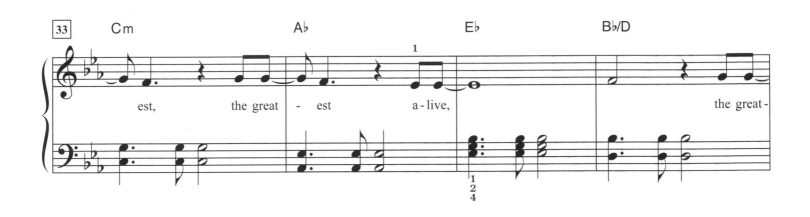

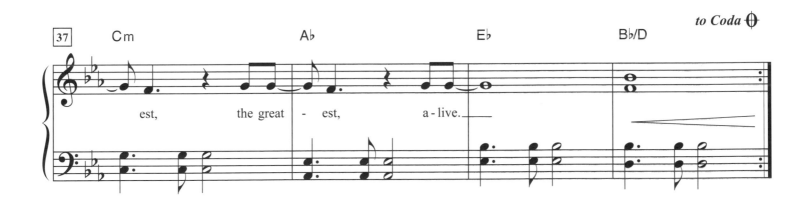

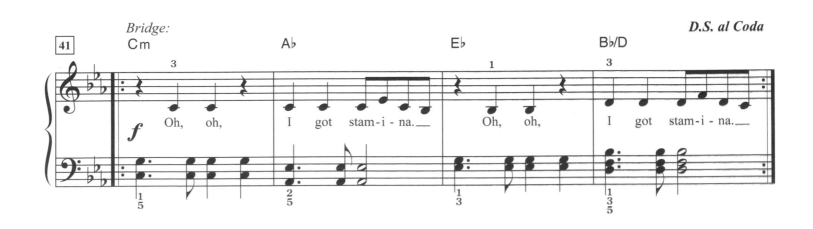

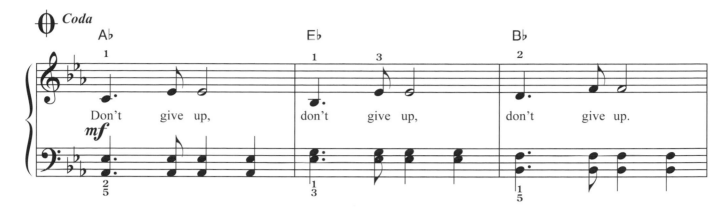

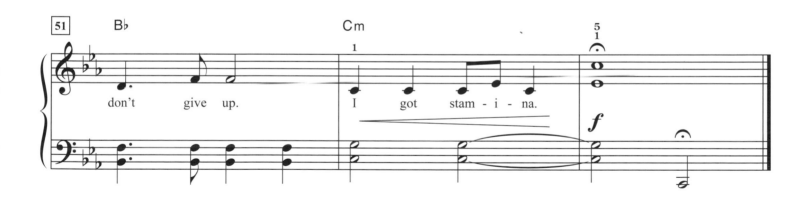

Verse 2:
Uh-oh, running out of breath, but I,
Oh, I, I got stamina.
Uh-oh, running now, I close my eyes,
But uh-oh, I got stamina.
And oh, yeah, I'm running through the waves of love,
But oh, oh, I got stamina.
And oh, yeah, I'm running and I've just enough,
And uh-oh, I got stamina.
(To Pre-Chorus:)

HEATHENS

Words and Music by Tyler Joseph
Arr. Dan Coates

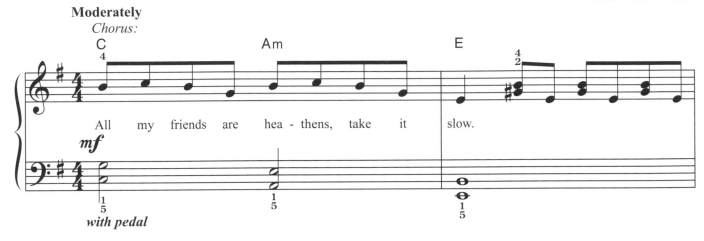

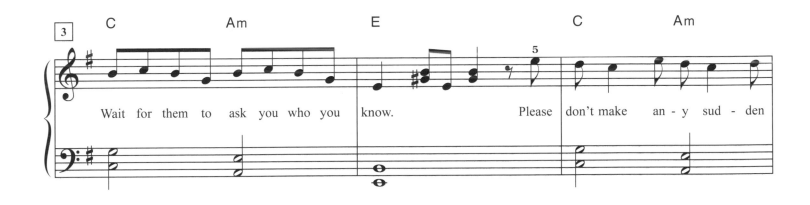

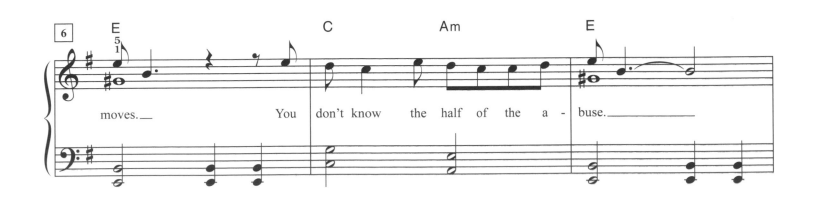

HOW FAR I'LL GO

(from *Moana*)

Words and Music by Lin-Manuel Miranda
Arr. Dan Coates

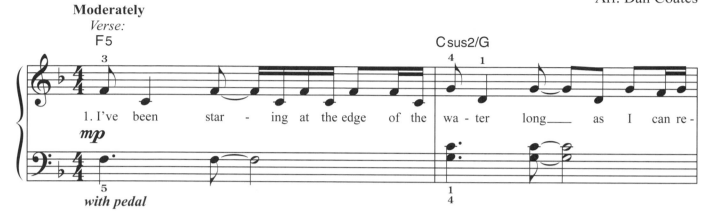

JUST LIKE FIRE

(from *Alice Through the Looking Glass*)

Words and Music by Oscar Holter,
Max Martin, Shellback and Alecia Moore
Arr. Dan Coates

Verse 2:
And people liked to laugh at you 'cause they are all the same, mm.
See I would rather we just go our different way than play the game, mm.
And no matter the weather, we can do it better,
You and me together, forever and ever.
We don't have to worry about a thing, about a thing, no.
(To Chorus:)

LOVE ON THE BRAIN

Words and Music by
Robyn Fenty, Joseph Angel and Fred Ball
Arr. Dan Coates

NEWT SAYS GOODBYE TO TINA / JACOB'S BAKERY

(from *Fantastic Beasts and Where to Find Them*)

Composed by James Newton Howard
Arr. Dan Coates

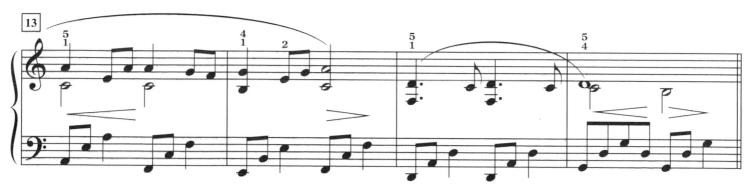

Moderate swing (♩♩ = ♪³♪)
"Jacob's Bakery"

simile

MIA & SEBASTIAN'S THEME

(from *La La Land*)

By Justin Hurwitz
Arr. Dan Coates

Moderately slow, expressively

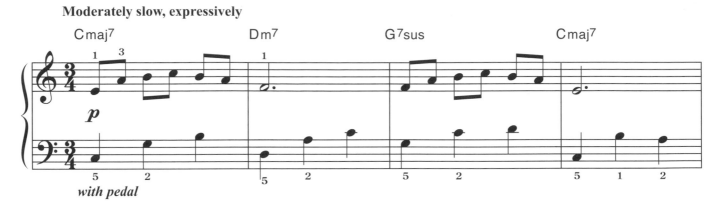

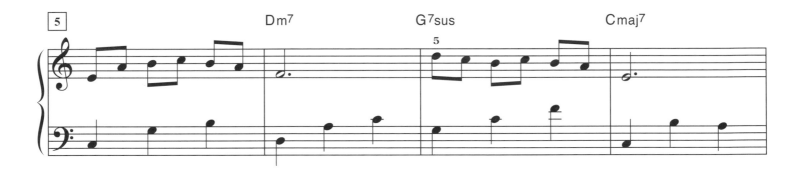

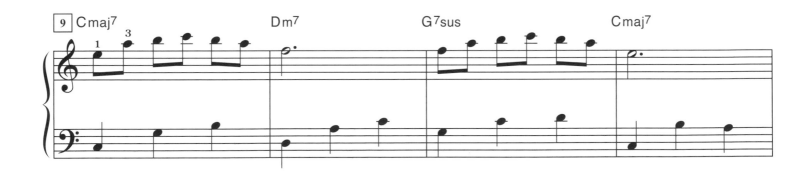

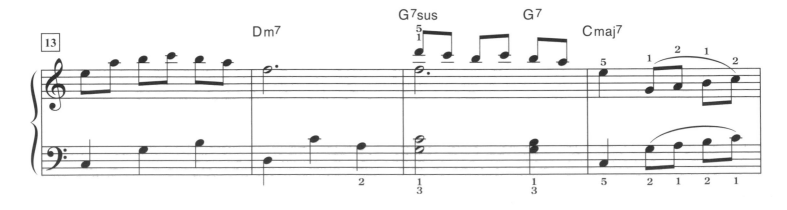

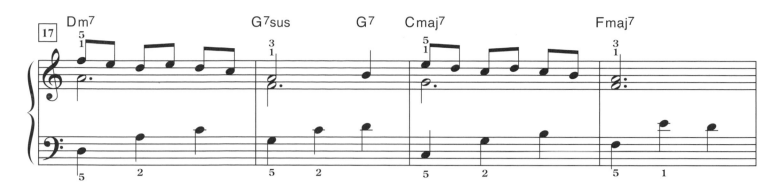

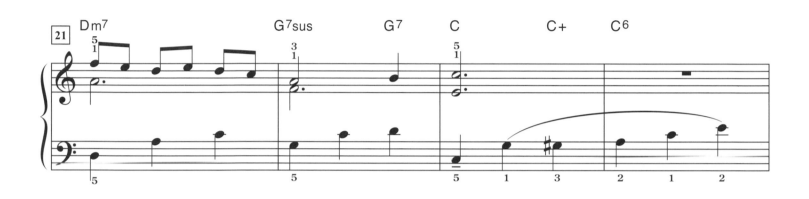

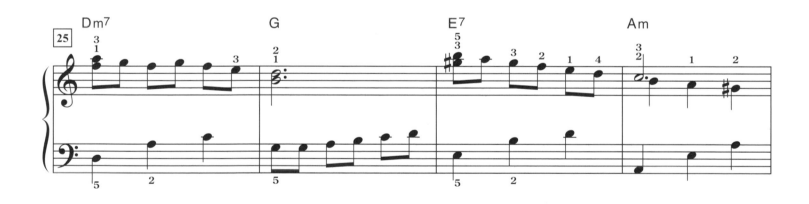

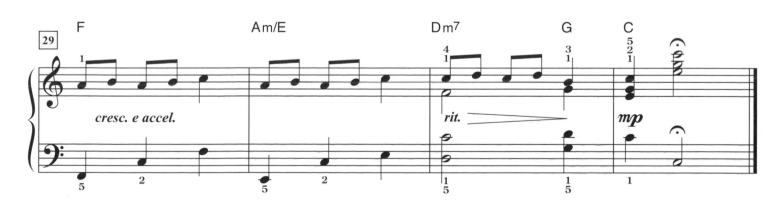

NOT TODAY

(from *Me Before You*)

Words and Music by
Daniel Reynolds, Daniel Platzman, Benjamin McKee,
Daniel Sermon and Mike Daly
Arr. Dan Coates

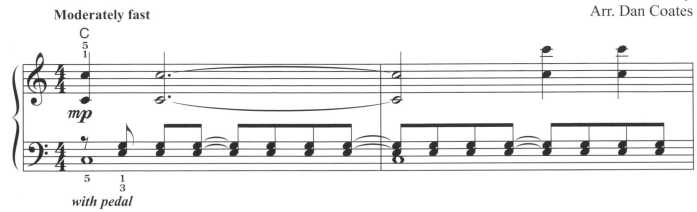

Pre-Chorus:

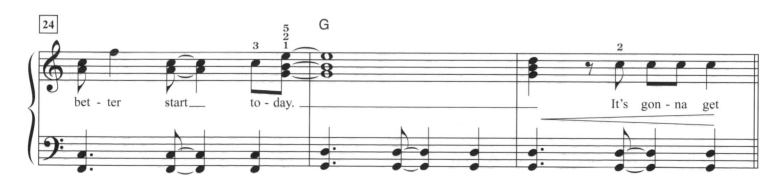

62

RIDE

Words and Music by Tyler Joseph
Arr. Dan Coates

SHAPE OF YOU

Words and Music by Kevin Briggs, Kandi Burruss,
Tameka Cottle, Ed Sheeran, Johnny McDaid and Steve Mac
Arr. Dan Coates

Verse 2:
One week in, we let the story begin,
We're going out on our first date,
You and me are thrifty so go all you can eat,
Fill up your bag and I fill up a plate.
We talk for hours and hours about the sweet and the sour
And how your family's doing O.K.
Leave and get in a taxi, then kiss in the back seat,
Tell the driver make the radio play.
And now I'm singing like
(To Pre-Chorus:)

SIDE TO SIDE

Words and Music by Ilya, Savan Kotecha, Max Martin,
Ariana Grande, Alex Kronlund and Onika Maraj
Arr. Dan Coates

STARVING

Words and Music by Anastasia Whiteacre, Robert McCurdy,
Christopher Petrosino, Kyle Trewartha and Michael Trewartha
Arr. Dan Coates

D.S. al Coda

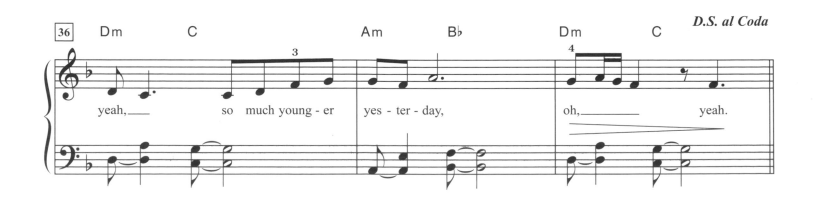

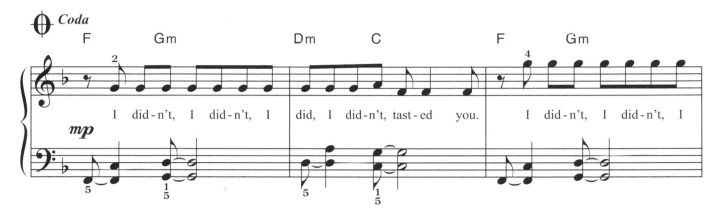

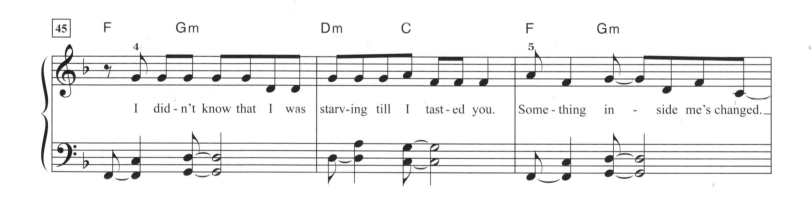

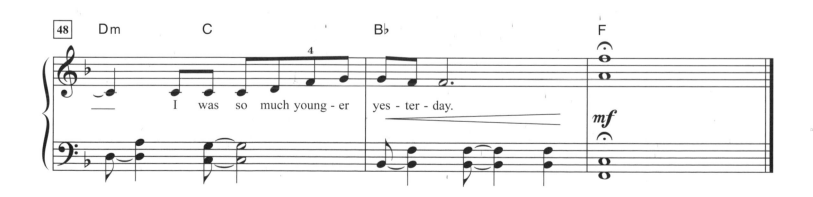

TEAR IN MY HEART

Words and Music by Tyler Joseph
Arr. Dan Coates